For
my daughter Amber

Love,
mother

JANE AUSTEN'S
LITTLE INSTRUCTION BOOK

by Jane Austen

Edited by Sophia Bedford-Pierce ◆ Design by Mullen & Katz

PETER PAUPER PRESS, INC.
WHITE PLAINS, NEW YORK

Copyright © 1995
Peter Pauper Press, Inc.
202 Mamaroneck Avenue
White Plains, NY 10601
All rights reserved
ISBN 0-88088-693-5
Printed in China
7 6

Table of Contents

Introduction

$\mathcal{E}$njoy this fine little collection and apply the sentiments expressed herein as they fit your daily life, or simply smile knowingly at Jane Austen's observations of human nature, a nature that does not seem to change, no matter what has come before—or after.

A mind lively and at ease can do with seeing nothing, and can see nothing that does not answer, wrote Austen in *Emma.* Indeed, the words fit the author well as she unrolls the scenery and the sights, sounds, and smells of the world of early nineteenth-century provincial England.

Jane Austen's Little Instruction Book has been borrowed with admiration from the pages of *Sense and Sensibility, Mansfield Park, Emma, Northanger Abbey, Persuasion,* and *Pride and Prejudice.* Sometimes fanciful and charming, always insightful, this volume offers a late twentieth-century selection of Ms. Austen's social observations. It includes chapters on women, men, their relationships with each other, some simple rules that prove to be timeless in their moral clarity, and a gathering of "life-lessons," often useful, sometimes more of her time than ours, but turned into entertainment by a keen mind wielding a smart pen.

If a woman *doubts* as to whether she should accept a man or not,
she certainly ought to refuse him. If she can hesitate as to "Yes,"
she ought to say "No," directly.

EMMA WOODHOUSE

Emma

What young lady . . . will reach the age of sixteen without
altering her name as far as she can?

Northanger Abbey

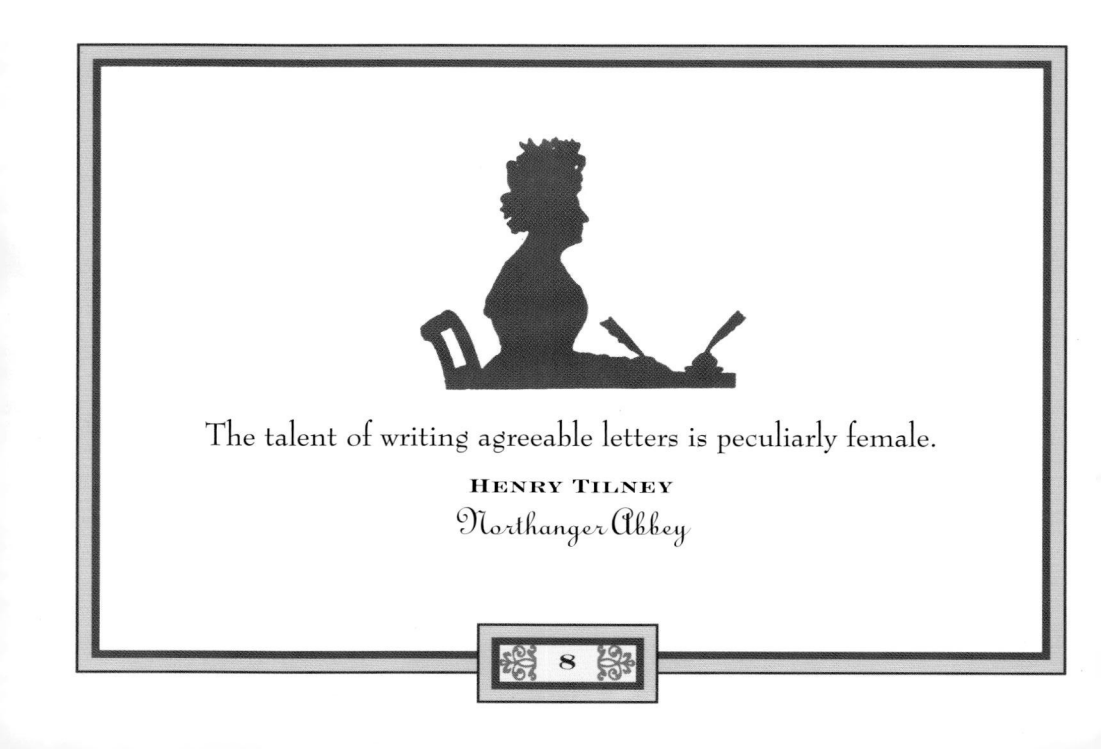

The talent of writing agreeable letters is peculiarly female.

HENRY TILNEY
Northanger Abbey

8

It sometimes happens that a woman is handsomer at twenty-nine
than she was ten years before; and, generally speaking,
if there has been neither ill-health nor anxiety, it is a time of life
at which scarcely any charm is lost.

Persuasion

9

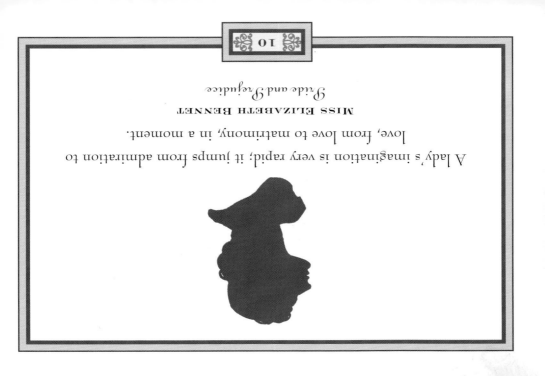

A lady's imagination is very rapid; it jumps from admiration to love, from love to matrimony, in a moment.

MISS ELIZABETH BENNET
Pride and Prejudice

When a young lady is to be a heroine, the perverseness of forty surrounding families cannot prevent her.

Northanger Abbey

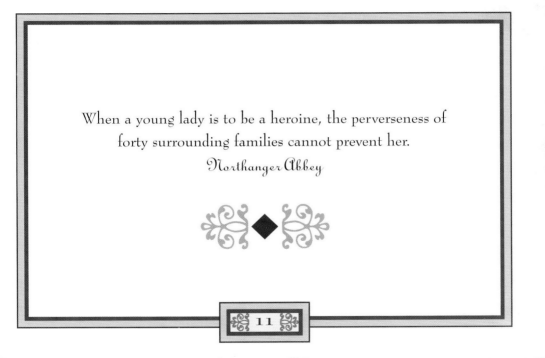

If a woman is partial to a man, and does not endeavour
to conceal it, he must find it out.

ELIZABETH

Pride and Prejudice

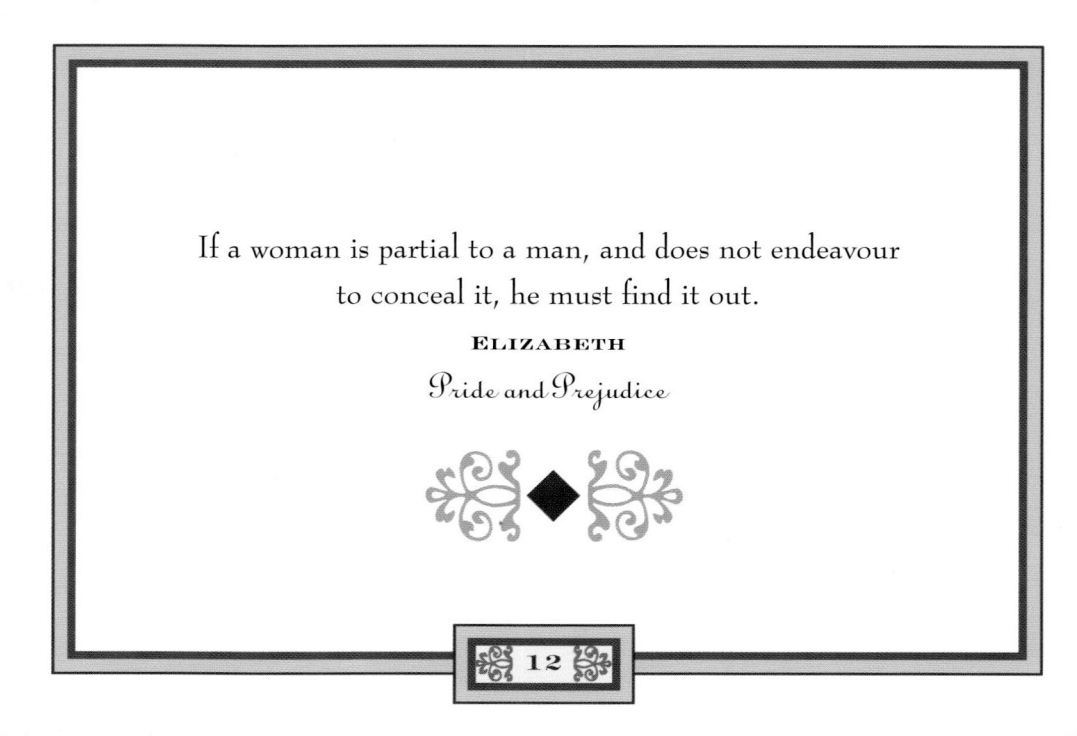

A woman is not to marry a man merely because she is asked,
or because he is attached to her.

EMMA

Emma

If the heroine of one novel be not patronised by the heroine
of another, from whom can she expect protection and regard?

Northanger Abbey

They (men) are very often amazingly impertinent, if you do not treat them with spirit, and make them keep their distance. . . . They give themselves such airs. They are the most conceited creatures in the world, and think themselves of so much importance!

ISABELLA THORPE

Northanger Abbey

It is always incomprehensible to a man, that a woman should ever refuse an offer of marriage. A man always imagines a woman to be ready for anybody who asks her.

EMMA

Emma

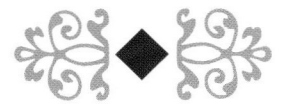

A man must have a very good opinion of himself
when he asks people to leave their own fireside . . . for the
sake of coming to see him.

JOHN KNIGHTLEY

Emma

Men never know when things are dirty or not.

Emma

Those men who do not choose to dance or marry themselves, have no business with the partners or wives of their neighbours. . . . Fidelity and complaisance are the principal duties of both.

JOHN THORPE

Northanger Abbey

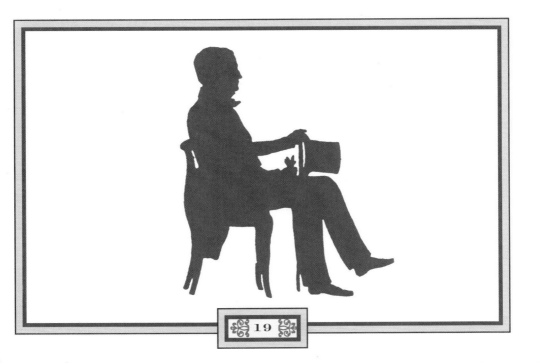

Relationships

If the dispositions of the parties are ever so well known to each other or ever so similar beforehand, it does not advance their felicity in the least. . . . it is better to know as little as possible of the defects of the person with whom you are to pass your life.

CHARLOTTE

Pride and Prejudice

One half of the world
cannot understand the pleasures of the other.

EMMA

Emma

◆ ◆ ◆ ◆ ◆ ◆ ◆ ◆

It is safer to leave people to their own devices . . .
Everybody likes to go their own way—to choose their
own time and manner of devotion.

FANNY PRICE

Mansfield Park

Nobody, who has not been in the interior of a family, can say
what the difficulties of any individual of that family may be.

EMMA

Emma

There is safety in reserve, but no attraction.
One cannot love a reserved person.

FRANK CHURCHILL

Emma

In every power of which taste is the foundation,
excellence is pretty fairly divided between the sexes.

CATHERINE MORLAND

Northanger Abbey

Of all horrid things leave-taking is the worst.

FRANK CHURCHILL

Emma

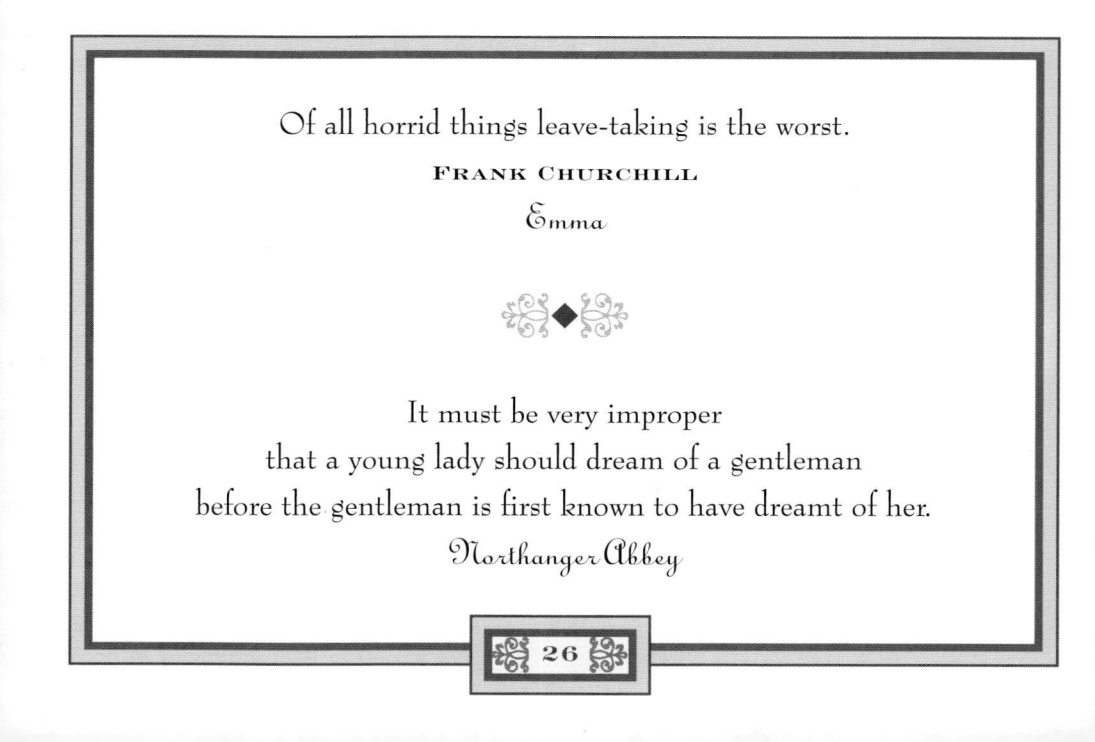

It must be very improper
that a young lady should dream of a gentleman
before the gentleman is first known to have dreamt of her.

Northanger Abbey

Vanity and pride are different things, though the words are often used synonymously. A person may be proud without being vain. Pride relates more to our opinion of ourselves, vanity to what we would have others think of us.

MARY

Pride and Prejudice

Nothing is more deceitful than the appearance of humility.
It is often only carelessness of opinion,
and sometimes an indirect boast.

MR. DARCY

Pride and Prejudice

Friendship is certainly the finest balm
for the pangs of disappointed love.
Northanger Abbey

Some Simple Rules

Perfect happiness, even in memory, is not common.

Emma

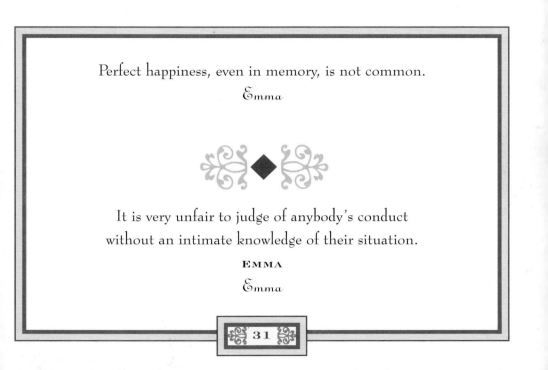

It is very unfair to judge of anybody's conduct
without an intimate knowledge of their situation.

EMMA

Emma

31

Separate esteem and love.

MRS. HENRY DASHWOOD

Sense and Sensibility

Every impulse of feeling should be guided
by reason; . . . exertion should always be in proportion
to what is required.

MARY

Pride and Prejudice

Remember where you are,
and do not run on in the wild manner
that you are suffered to do at home.

MRS. BENNET

Pride and Prejudice

Do not let us be frightened from a good deed by a trifle.

MRS. NORRIS

Mansfield Park

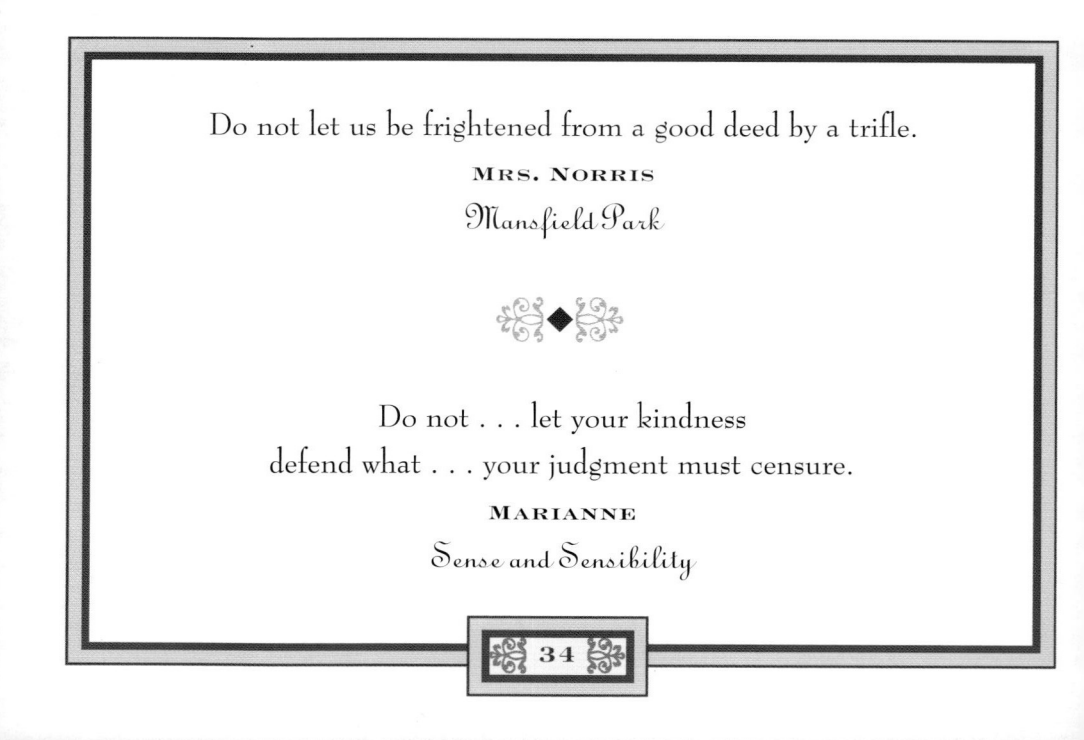

Do not . . . let your kindness
defend what . . . your judgment must censure.

MARIANNE

Sense and Sensibility

A lucky guess is never merely luck.
There is always some talent in it.

MR. KNIGHTLEY

Emma

◆ ◆ ◆ ◆ ◆ ◆ ◆ ◆

There is one thing . . . which a man can always do,
if he chooses, and that is, his duty;
not by manœuvering and finessing,
but by vigour and resolution.

MR. KNIGHTLEY

Emma

Where health is at stake nothing else should be considered.

MR. WOODHOUSE
Emma

❖

A mind lively and at ease can do with seeing nothing,
and can see nothing that does not answer.

Emma

Success supposes endeavour.

MR. KNIGHTLEY

Emma

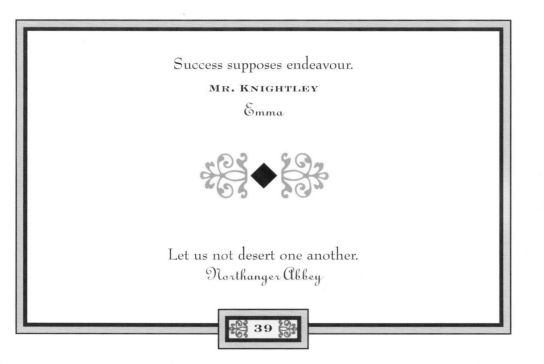

Let us not desert one another.

Northanger Abbey

Everything nourishes what is strong already.

MISS ELIZABETH BENNET

Pride and Prejudice

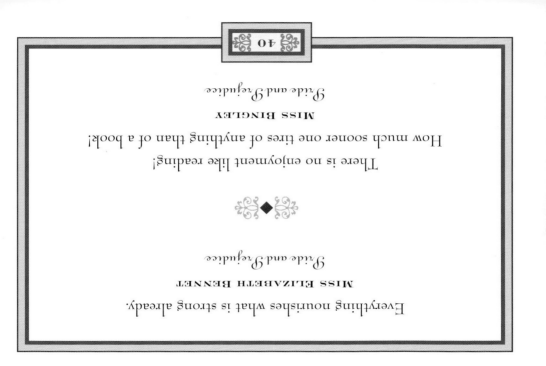

There is no enjoyment like reading!
How much sooner one tires of anything than of a book!

MISS BINGLEY

Pride and Prejudice

41

Life Lessons

A man who has nothing to do with his own time
has no conscience in his intrusion on that of others.

MARIANNE

Sense and Sensibility

The distance is nothing when one has a motive.

MR. BENNET

Pride and Prejudice

People do not die of little trifling colds.

MRS. BENNET

Pride and Prejudice

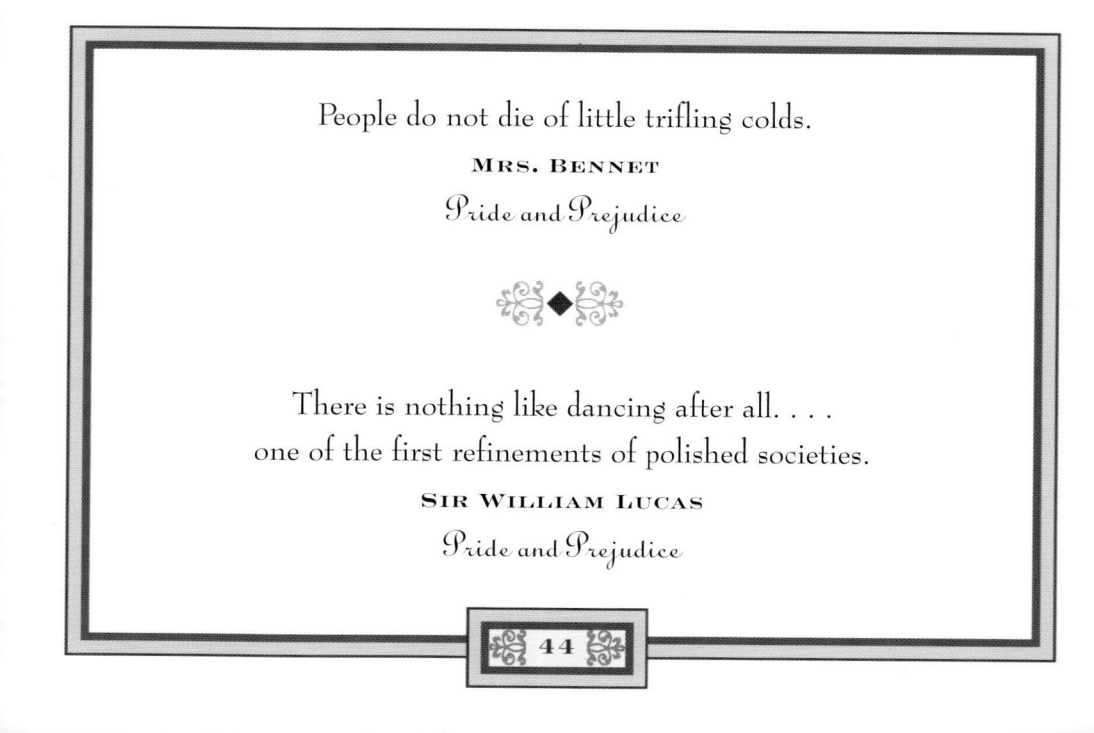

There is nothing like dancing after all. . . .
one of the first refinements of polished societies.

SIR WILLIAM LUCAS

Pride and Prejudice

No one can be really esteemed accomplished who does not greatly surpass what is usually met with.

Pride and Prejudice

Those persons who fancy themselves very important,
and never open their mouths, quite mistake the matter.

MRS. BENNET

Pride and Prejudice

❖

A person who can write a long letter with ease,
cannot write ill.

Pride and Prejudice

The power of doing anything with quickness
is always much prized by the possessor, and often without
any attention to the imperfection of the performance.

MR. DARCY

Pride and Prejudice

47

The wisest and the best of men—
nay, the wisest and best of their actions may be rendered
ridiculous by a person whose first object in life is a joke.

MR. DARCY

Pride and Prejudice

They who are good-natured when children,
are good-natured when they grow up.

MRS. REYNOLDS

Pride and Prejudice

To sit in the shade on a fine day
and look upon verdure,
is the most perfect refreshment.

FANNY PRICE

Mansfield Park

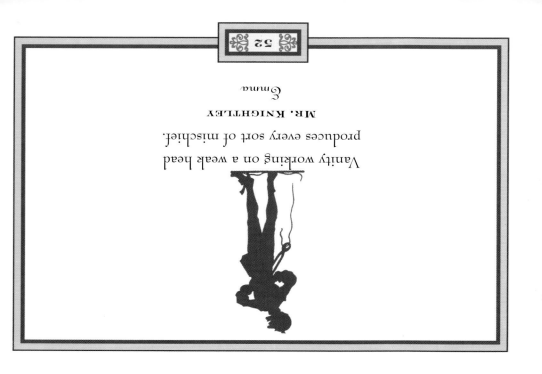

Vanity working on a weak head
produces every sort of mischief.

MR. KNIGHTLEY

Emma

(Those) who must be pleased . . .
are sometimes to be pleased only by a good many sacrifices.

MR. WESTON

Emma

Where little minds belong to rich people in authority . . .
they have a knack of swelling out
till they are quite as unmanageable as great ones.

EMMA

Emma

56

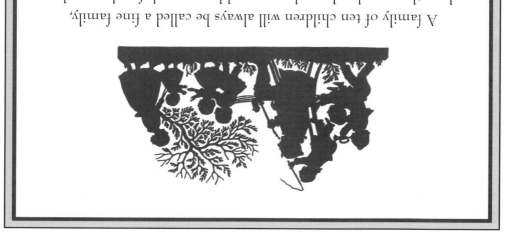

A family of ten children will always be called a fine family,
where there are heads, and arms, and legs enough for the number.

Northanger Abbey

Strange things may be generally accounted for
if their cause be fairly searched out.
Northanger Abbey

The liveliest effusions of wit and humour
are conveyed to the world in the best chosen language.
Northanger Abbey

58

Dress is at all times a frivolous distinction,
and excessive solicitude about it often destroys its own aim.

Northanger Abbey

How quick come the reasons
for approving what we like!

Persuasion

People always live for ever
when there is any annuity to be paid them.

MRS. JOHN (FANNY) DASHWOOD

Sense and Sensibility

Vanity is a weakness indeed.
But pride—where there is a real superiority of mind,
pride will be always under good regulation.

MR. DARCY

Pride and Prejudice

Better be without sense than to misapply it. . . .

MR. KNIGHTLEY

Emma

61

It is that dreadful habit of opening the windows,
letting in cold air upon heated bodies,
which . . . does the mischief.

FRANK CHURCHILL
Emma

In a country neighbourhood
you move in a very confined and
unvarying society.

MR. DARCY

Pride and Prejudice

64

Silly things do cease to be silly
if they are done by sensible people in an impudent way.
Wickedness is always wickedness, but folly is not always folly.
It depends upon the character of those who handle it.

EMMA
Emma